PRAISE FOR *IN HER JAWS*

'Taylor's poems possess a talismanic quality. With lyric sorcery, she conjures encounters with a chorus of wild creatures: spectres and lovers, selves and others.' Nidhi Zak / Aria Eipe

'In these haunting, simmering metamorphoses, Rosamund Taylor's imagination is both intrepid and tender. Spanning the erotic and the traumatic, these poems root through the fibrous dark of our psyche.' Seán Hewitt

'This is a debut that leaves bite marks in the most erotic and intoxicating sense.' Victoria Kennefick

'Taylor's language, form and imagery exhibit a remarkable freshness, resulting in work that manages to create a space between the uncanny and the familiar ... This is the Irish lyric tradition queered in the manifold and finest meanings of that word ... We are all the richer for it.' Paul Maddern

'A book of astonishments whose poems gaze towards the night sky and all that stirs in the dark below, swooping the reader through mysteries of desire and discovery. Taylor's voice is by turns tender, sharp, luminous; her poems are wondrous.' Doireann Ní Ghríofa

'The reader travels wild paths in skilled hands. Taylor's voice is evocative, assured and unforgettable. This is absolutely exquisite.' Deirdre Sullivan

'*In Her Jaws* is by turns delicate and fierce; holding the reader gently in its muzzle, where we thrill to the awareness of teeth against our carotid.' Jessica Traynor

Rosamund Taylor won the *London Magazine* Poetry Prize 2020 and the Mairtín Crawford Award for Poetry 2017. Widely published, her work has recently appeared in *Butcher's Dog, Magma, Mslexia, The Rialto* and *Poetry Ireland Review*. A selection of her poems is included in *Queering the Green: Post-2000 Queer Irish Poetry* (The Lifeboat Press).

In Her Jaws

In Her Jaws

Rosamund Taylor

BANSHEE
PRESS

First published 2022 by
Banshee Press
www.bansheelit.com

A CIP record for this title is available from the British Library.

Grateful acknowledgement is made to Penguin Books Limited for permission to reproduce material from *Lolly Willowes* by Sylvia Townsend Warner. Copyright © the Estate of Sylvia Townsend Warner, 1926, published by Chatto & Windus 1926, Penguin Classics, 2020.

Banshee Press gratefully acknowledges
the financial assistance of the Arts Council.

ISBN: 978-1-8383126-4-0

Set in Palatino by Eimear Ryan
Cover design by Anna Morrison
Printed and bound in Great Britain by Clays Ltd, Elcograf S.p.A.

For Milena

Contents

That's why we become witches: to show our scorn of pretending life's a safe business, to satisfy our passion for adventure.

– Sylvia Townsend Warner, *Lolly Willowes*

In Her Jaws

I Met My Other Self

I met my other self
in Knocksink Wood. She wore grey.
Sweet chestnuts and hornbeams
were losing their last leaves
as morning light stretched shadows.
She busied herself in the mulch,
searching for something – a bulb, a nut.
I made her shiver
as though she'd unearthed a blue tit,
its mouth glued shut by frost.

I was a week of rain:
raw bark, mud in her mouth,
nights too wet to sleep through.
I stepped towards her –
she sprang up the closest oak.
She was more air than body,
her fur full of light.

The Light Comes in the Name of the Voice

i.m. Jeanne d'Arc (1412–1431)

First the ash pile, white, fine wood ash,
grimy ice, a grey noon. The pigs.
Frost lacing the leaves. The girl
with itchy thighs, cold nose. Then
this moment. The voice.
The light.

The light.
It did not flow like a shaft of sunlight
muted in water; it wasn't like snow,
snow at dawn, the white flecks
on a fox's tail as it scrambles in snow ferns.
Nor like the flash of a stoat at dusk
overcoming a rabbit bigger than itself
(though, like the stoat, it held everything
in its jaws). It wasn't even like moonlight,
being thirteen, warm in a moonlit room, moon
so full and bright it lies in long white beams, white
shadows on the skin, skin melting into shadows
as though there is no longer any space
between self and moon. The light

was only like itself
just as she was only Jeanne. Her breath
a shape in the frost. Then the light,
the voice: always now. Wordless and complete.

She was questioned. At her trial they asked
where does your voice come from
do you hear it like you hear my voice
when do you hear it do you hear it now
does it echo   She could not answer.
There were no answers, as there had
been no songs, no angels, no shadows. Only light,

the girl transformed by light. After the trial
it seemed to her that the light had always been full
of the smell of herself burning: her bursting lungs,
her fried skin. The questions already licked
her arms; behind the voice, her white ashes –

and somewhere she still knelt by the pigsty, hands tense
as if searching for a sword.

Old Quarry

a child in my polyester uniform   I came here
seeking a little vixen   imagining I'd tame her

webs warped   over the loom of brambles
      hid   beer cans and plastic bags

the all-night garage hummed   petrol-smell
    settled in the leaf mould

but I listened to the conversations   trees hold
    the rippling of whispers   from branch to root
      layering through leaves

pretending   I was a mushroom
    growing in beech mast   in rhythm
      with the grey-and-tan striped spiders

I was sure one day   the fox   her tidy face
would peek   from skeletons of purple loosestrife

    and we'd play in fuchsia together

instead   underneath the wild   crab apples
a man   displayed   his phallus to me

I Hear That They Call Life

after Paul Celan

Although I wasn't sane, I could blend
with tourists on the Royal Mile.
I fingered Loch Ness Monster hats,
St Andrew's crosses, hid in quiet wynds.
Regulars pushed through throngs
using Tesco bags as battering rams
while the transient and footsore
preferred shortbread at Thistle Do Nicely
and watching cooks mix molten
fat and sugar in the Fudge Kitchen.
Licking condensation and cinnamon,
I'd wait by the window in Caffè Nero
for a married woman, who'd twist
my long hair round her hand and tug.
In kirkyards, I found refuge
with brittle manticores, resting for hours
where knapweed and mallow grew ragged
around fallen gravestones. The many ghosts
were a comfort – plague dead, Burke and Hare,
throngs of cattle, horses. I saw them all.
I was 20, then 21 – I never slept,
my eyes burned red as a devil's;
I watched the sun blaze and die
and wake on my window,
thinking Thistle Do Nicely, this'll do ...

The Names We Called You Meant Nothing to Me

We shouted *witch*
but inside I said meadowsweet, hollyhock, clover.

We said we'd peel off your skin
but I dreamed of you taking me:
the sky let you go and you landed
between laurel trees at the graveyard gate.
You covered my mouth. Your hand dry as a moth.

In bed I imagined
the smell of your cloak: lanolin and cobwebs;
the smell of the skin at your throat,
sweet resin, sweat and woodsmoke. I was so tender.

At harvest, the village set a fire and we chanted
crone, hag, Satan's whore. I danced with you:
our shadows in the flames and soft ash,
the heat catching our faces, our arms.
We were red and gold and impervious.

We didn't burn the oak
though its roots circled our bonfire.
It smelled green; it grew lichen. In the morning
I found you there hung from a noose.
Your feet without their shoes.
Your toes blue and small.

I was afraid, and then I remembered our names for you.
I began with *witch*.

A Particular Scent of Salt

It's warm enough to sip coffee
and sit by the sea watching wagtails
dip in and out of clumps of bladderwrack
when I feel him against my legs and groin.

– Once again I'm trying to escape,
my face pressed so hard
into the locker door that the vent
leaves three horizontal lines on my cheek.

What colour are your knickers today?
He pushes my skirt up, up, up,
over knees, crotch, hips, waist.
The heat of his breath. Smell

of crisps, eggs. Everyone laughs
but later, in class, another girl
presses tissues into my hand.
A long time ago now. I saw him once,

bearded, smiling as he held his child
and spun her up and out in an arc.
She laughed, undaunted by gravity,
by the air under her feet.

Portrait of My Anxiety as an Imp

My imp comes with me everywhere I go.
She tugs my hair and curls her silky tail
so tight around my neck she stops airflow;
when she's nervous she chews my nails
until they bleed. She's afraid on busy streets,
in classrooms and in pubs. She clawed free
at the concert hall: she nipped people's feet
and howled as violins and cellos rose in key.

Long ago, she survived in woods and fenland,
she hid from falcons and relentless bears,
sleeping in pine needles, shivering downwind.
But now she's safe indoors. Foxes are scared,
eagles poisoned: she still won't believe she's fine,
there are no jaws waiting to snap her spine.

Household Gods

Every night my mother leaves an offering,
her torch beam falling on the icy pond
and skeletons of thistle. The fox gulps
chicken carcasses, curdled custard.
The scent of fat alone sustained Greek gods
but he is more mouth than presence,
known by a coarse-furred tail
or a stink under the brambles. In spring
he demands the night's attention,
rasping cries oddly human. My mother
depends on him for a rustle in the elder
that is more than the wind.

And when she is a fox, my mother
smells of raw earth and vinegar.
She paces around the apple trees,
digs under the shed and compost heap.
I wake to her singing – fox songs
without words but in a familiar cadence.
I am drawn to her silhouette,
the movement of her haunches, her nose,
but cannot speak her name: in the dark,
she is a wild thing I might spook.
I will never really know her,
this sure-footed vixen.

I Mapped the Heavens

i.m. Caroline Herschel (1750–1848)

On Surviving Typhoid Fever

Mother never forgave me for being alive.
The typhoid made me stooped, my legs short
so I couldn't marry. But my hands were quick.
As I trod icy streets, I looked up –

sometimes tripping over frozen excrement.
I remembered my brother's hand
leading mine. *See the planets*, he said
that's Jupiter, and there's Mars, there,

among those constellations. So I walked
with the Seven Sisters, their stern faces,
or met Orion, heard his gruff laugh
as he looped his belt round my waist.

All fancy – I read until my head turned.
I couldn't resist the papers my brother sent
on telescopes, solar winds, and stars.
I never slept much, but when I did, I dreamed.

At five, I woke to morning stars,
and broke flinty ice on water buckets. I brought
Mother hot milk in bed. She pinched me,
but I never squeaked. She liked it when I did.

I was paying her back for my illness, the days
spent in bed, the man I couldn't wed, the woman
I couldn't be. I stitched my piecework, fingers
rubbed raw, and in candlelight,

I sang to myself in my clear soprano.
I put names of comets, of Jupiter's moons,
and celestial distances, to familiar tunes.
My mind held the whole scope of the sky.

A Descent

... they could not lift me without leaving nearly two ounces of my
flesh behind.

　　　　　　　　　　　　　　　　　　　– Caroline Herschel

all day I grind glass　　to lenses
　　　　trapping them　　　　in our telescopes
with my scarred hands　　　　　　while all night

I map the heavens
　　　　my brother calls out each star to me
his eye at the lens　　　　I don't look up

moving from my map　　　only to soothe
　　　　his cramped fingers
as his students　　　fumble their calculations

my head　　　is so full of stars
　　　　it expands like the galaxy　　　　I'm
slipping　　　on icy mud　　　　hooked

　　　　to the largest telescope in England
by a bracket's spiked edge
my face and chest press　　　into iron

the sky turns white
　　　　each familiar star　　　a point of black
bold as crows　　　on a summer day

comets dart like minnows in shimmering pools
      and each is mine
mine to learn   with my own eyes and hands

to chart   on my maps
      I am the centre of the heavens
of the white sky   such light   such light   and I

am lifted free   two white ounces
      of my flesh ooze on the telescope
my brother clings to my hand   sways

at the blood   saying   *Astronomy perhaps*
is best left to men   tonight I leave him
      I take up my pen

We Become Witches

Astronomy is no better than witchcraft,
Mother said. Books frightened her.
Perhaps she's right: only witches
would come in January to this frozen field
when the moon is a sliver and eyes burn.
I am a molehill of wool, featureless,
chanting star charts to myself like a charm,
investigating mathematics instead of fine sewing
or the downy shape of a baby's head.
      A black door swings on its hinges:
      with my telescope, I walk
      on Pegasus's wings. I don't see witches,
      no hags boiling curses, no virgins scrying
      in pools of silver blood, not even here
      in the stars. But it feels like sorcery
      when I unstitch the sky, unpicking nebulae,
      finding a white tail, and another.
      I see myself, here and here: I am a comet,
      my orbit long, inscrutable, easy to overlook.

Sandra

When I was a day patient
Sandra took me to the tea room
and showed me where nurses
hid the good biscuits – wafers
and chocolate fingers. She told me
if I was hearing voices
to hold my phone to my ear
and no one would guess
who I was talking to. *It used
to be much harder to hide*, she said,
*you'd have to wait till you found
a phone booth. By then the voice
might be scalding your brain.*
She went outside to smoke,
levering herself along on her walker.
It was summer, the sky cloudless
and I ate a biscuit as a wasp
fussed at the window. After
weeks of whispers from shadows
and seeing hanged men in stairwells,
I worried I was just like Sandra.
Holding my hot cup, I took comfort:
despite her bowed knees, her drool,
her one eye was clear as god's.

Fearing Death Is a Kind of Joy

Holding a broken bottle
to my throat he told me
not to move. So I didn't.
I was eager to live:
each breath as bitter
and brilliant as diving
into the sea. My feet
in black school shoes
bounced against the bottom
of the van, each beat
a victory boom: *I am*
alive. I am alive.
Then he threw me outside –

limping, stained,
I began to wonder whether
living had really been
worth it. I could have cut
my own neck on the glass.
Every moment was opaque
as treacle and I
became a Mexican tetra,
a blind fish living
in cave pools on bat shit
and rotten moss, desperate
joy turned
to torpor.

When I Was Twelve

When I was twelve, I did not conceive
but still the child appears. Sometimes
a turnip child, made from roots and onions,

her face, white as the inside
of a chestnut shell, only an impression
of ears and nose, but perfect.

Sometimes a coal-cellar child, she comes
sparkling with dust, her eyebrows gold,
her tongue made of fossil ferns,

her cries the sounds of embers
spitting on a hearth. Or a mushroom child:
when I squeeze her, she spills spores

like a puffball, and smells
of late-autumn orchards. She's cursed
to never grow up, to remind me

I never quickened, never grew heavy
and limp with nausea, never split
open like a nut. A toy child,

made from satin and cotton grown soft
with time; now when she screams
I don't curse her: I hold her to my breast.

Jack-in-the-Box

autism spectrum disorder, at age 20

I am a gorilla   but caged
with flamingos and macaws
      such colour!   I cover
my eyes   with leaves

in the mulch   I become small
      between wall   and tree trunk
woodlice walk   over my ankles

I am learning   not to make a fuss
      putting my hands in my mouth
      so screams press
against them   a jack-in-the-box
drumming his head   against his wooden lid

too old to be afraid
      of supermarkets   where tomatoes
pulse with fluorescence

      or of the vacuum cleaner's roar
      shattering my   skull and teeth
like eggshell

by the front door
      a harvestman   translates
his jumble of legs and wings
      into a French-lace shadow

my only ally
      like me   he waits
for   a parenthesis
      (   )

For Pickle

When I cry he cries,
erupts from the ironing pile,
bulldozes onto my lap,
presses triangular face
and dense body against me
until we soothe each other
with purrs and pets.
I'm brought back
to the times I'd plan
to hurt myself.
I turned the key,
found razor, gauze,
while he pressed himself
against the door, paws
skittering underneath,
frantic to barrel his way to me.
Often I'd relent.
He'd climb my clothes, purr,
burrow into me,
could not, would not,
let me hurt myself.

Since the Wound Occurred

I take it these were self-inflicted.
I lift the left arm as he asks, nod,
lift the right. He doesn't touch –
his tiny torch unthreads me,
unwinds the white lines on rib cage,
upper arm, thigh, hip. Fear pools –
I smell musk from my pubis, armpits.
And this one? Has it always looked like this?
I reply: *Since the wound occurred ...*
as though I am not responsible.
We'll have to take it off –
an uneven scar, dirty red.
Six years since I hurt myself –

I was far outside my skin,
made of driftwood, not bone.
Waves forced me back to shore
then out once more; I struck cliffs, rocks.
I spoke the language of kittiwakes,
knew only that I was alive.
The paper on the bed beneath me
crinkles and sticks. I stumble
into shirt, socks, button myself back up.
Smell of cigarettes breezes
through the window. Two voices:
– I'm destroyed with the wait.
– You don't come in here
        for the good of your health.

The Psychopomp and the Last Word

The smell imbued everything –
we inhaled popcorn as lions
crunched femurs and scapulas,
drizzle beading their fur. We hunted it,
wanting to wrap cold hands
around warm cones of corn. Crickets
rustled in the roof of the reptile house.
The chameleon was a psychopomp
luring me to Hades, the world
no more than oil slick on a puddle.
We didn't find popcorn or even sandwiches,
but discovered the source of the scent:
musk of a white-whiskered creature,
size of a black Labrador, astride a branch.
She consumed grapes with the deliberation
of Henry James at a garden party
while looking at us as though we were
in her dream. A *binturong* –
we read her name, the last known word
of an extinct language. The world
forgets more than I can imagine.
I pressed hands to mist-cold glass,
stole into her thoughts and drowsed
in a leaf-dark forest, fig juice
overspilling my jaws.

The Space You Take

After Prop *by Jenny Saville, oil on canvas, 1993*

I'm fourteen, bewildered by the gallery,
when I find you. Your canvas fills a whole wall.
Your knee is large as my head.

Your knee – its dusty pink, its rose,
its rivers of vein.
I've seen Rubens and Titian, but you –

I'm afraid you'll be censored.
Your spread of thigh, your pubic mound,
pillow of belly, mouthful of navel –

you make yourself look larger than you are,
you're not languorous: you're smug.
Someone will cover you in black plastic,

say that you're too much. I'm your supplicant
standing in your temple asking
for more –

mango-toothed straight from the skin,
nectar dripping over my lips,
down my chin and neck.

Survivor of the Eruption

she's always known it's dangerous to live below the volcano
everyone says so [1]

she also knows it's
       dangerous to leave the village
       to walk alone through terracotta shadows
       steal wine   wake with sore thighs
       to scream when she's whipped

and it's dangerous not to have parents
she's a goat walking to the altar

today her stomach clenches
clenches   she smells blood
as she darts along the muddy riverbed

above her   smoke changes colour
the earth sighs   *listen*
the mountain writes onto the sky

all at once she knows how small she is   her face

---

[1]   this soil is made of ash
has always been made of ash
is fertile because of ash

a star on a moonless night
as the fire opens the mountain

lava	ash clouds [2]
she's dead	she must be
she keeps walking	ash settles
on her face	around her eyes
her lungs cook	and rasp
thighs rough	with blood
nothing to drink	how long
has she walked	it's so dark
alone	she's always been alone

---

[2]   Pyroclastic flow   mixes molten rock
and gas. It eats crops,   sets vines alight,
engulfs houses,   encasing bread ovens
and butchers,   whole villas, their
frescos, tablecloths;   it swallows
children's clapping games,   names of
their dogs. It cannot be outrun.   At
night, pyroclastic flow   glows red,
glows for miles,   yellow lights spill
from the mountain;   from far away the
red is comforting   like a night light
or embers in   the grate throwing
familiar shades   over bedroom walls.

she crawls into the mossy-wet space under rocks
                    dead earthworms
                              millipedes
                    desiccated lizards

she screams when the men find her
her: smoke-streaked   blood-crusted [3]

not a reliable witness

we saw fire smoke Pompeii engulfed
you shouldn't be so close to the volcano   always knew
it was dangerous

---

[3]   Menstrual fluid is rich with nutrients,
soft,   a cushion for an absent baby.
It carries   no toxins, as clean as blood,
darker red. In water   red clots open
upwards, a shoal of curls   like
anemones' tentacles   or seaweed in a
rock pool.   It hurts now, like a small
birth   the body opening to expunge
unneeded tissue.   Vulnerable:
she is a wound;   she is not wounded.

much later

            a basin of water   reflects stars
her thighs washed brown   scratched   but clean
the sound of water at night   chuckle of frogs

she drinks   water warm as blood
she doesn't speak

a hand on her cheek   a voice
child   *it happens to all of us*

Dörchen

i.m. Dora Richter (1891–1933)

Dörchen, if I could, I'd give you a day off.
Woman's work is not kind to the hands –
hot water swells and reddens fingers,
potato peelers nick the knuckles,

and in the evenings, you sew when you sit,
darning socks, mending doctors' coats.
You sing with the other women –
rounds of folk songs you learnt as children.

I'd like to invite you here to a deckchair
on a sunny evening after a wet day
while ferns unscroll and the wind smells
of three-cornered leek and wild mint.

Sit down, I'd say. *You're my guest.*
Would you like sekt or prosecco?
If you let me, I'd roll the stockings
off your tired feet, and rub your soles,

swollen from standing for too long.
As the birds began their evening song,
you'd relax. I'd kneel there, looking up at you.
Tell me about yourself. Tell me everything.

The Polish for Beetroot Is Burak

Never pick ones with wrinkled skin.
I watch each movement
as your mother peels them,
her upward strokes, red
soaking into nail beds. In the sink
she heaps piles of purple skin,
then the grater's *scratch-scratch.*
She serves them raw
with lemon and sunflower oil.
The salad on the table like evidence
of a murder.
            I have to learn
not to be afraid of red; red flashes
at the tip of our tongues, and later
staining our urine. Or the taste –
sweet as apples but scented
with turned earth, mud on a spade,
new shoots pushing through rain.
I think we're sharing a language
until, through you, she says,
The Irish don't understand beetroot:
you choose stale ones, boil them to mush.

On Deciding to Read Emma

On the title page of *Emma*
I find my great-grandfather's initials
and the year: 1944. It's warped, salt-stained –
I picture him reading in faltering light

on the mailboat from Dún Laoghaire
to Holyhead as the sea swells,
clenching a cigarette in his uneasy mouth.
So little of the past survives –

scraps are blown into my life
like clothes from someone else's washing line.
There's a stack of shell-shaped bowls
in the kitchen, perhaps a century old,

and I see my nose, broad and blunt,
repeated on hazy figures in undated photos.
All Milena has from her grandmother
is a pair of earrings, gold tinged red by copper,

and shadows of things unvoiced.
One evening in December, tree lit,
we find her great-grandfather –
his picture preserved online.

Left profile, right profile, and facing front,
his head shaved, scalp gnarled, eyes sunk,
and a record of his death in 1941
after three months in Auschwitz.

His profession: farmer.
Later, Milena rests her head
in my lap as I read *Emma*.
The cover falls off in my hands.

Postcard From Killarney

Irish Citizenship Ceremony, 2018

Outside Mallow train station
Milena practises the oath
she'll swear to the Irish State
A thin rain works into our eyes,
under our tongues. Around us
languages overlap –
Urdu, Cantonese, Arabic, Czech.

On the bus to Killarney,
we crowd three to a row.
I press cold face to cold window.
Mist rolls into mist,
brown valleys whisper past us
hushed in leafless birches.
Milena grips my hand.

At the convention centre,
queues coil back and forth
through the car park. Water
sloshes inside my boots.
I'm tempted to join
the Romanian family
nestling under five umbrellas.

I used to ask Milena
if she missed Gorzów
but as she rests her head
on my shoulder, I know her answer.

A small boy hurtles into our knees.
We laugh, and steady him.
Two questions echo all around –

Where did you come from?
How long did you wait?

Ursa Major

i.m. Władysław Zwolak (1924–1980)

in 1949 he walked home from Siberia
    all his teeth fell out

as he walked   he forgot   everything
    kasha   plums in a saucepan   me
the children   the farm
he forgot   everything   except

his feet

        his shoes
        fell
        to pieces
toenails blackened   one   by one
a relief when he eased   the nail   from the toe
    and the blood blister   swelled

his nose and fingertips oozed   he cursed the ache in his guts

          the bear's paws broke
                the crust of snow
     snowlight   revealed the curve of her back

   no words   patterns of footfalls
     black water
          and her hot stink
                erasing him
    sound of her teeth on bone

he waited to be eaten

his wife told the children
       that he'd died in Siberia

             he navigated by the great bear

                 unlike other constellations
               she never dips below the rim of sky
      as he walked he
            became pine and moonlight

    the great she-bear shook stardust from her fur

Milk

That night,
          hunger was unbearable.
I climbed out of bed. My legs
          were almost translucent –
          they never saw sun.

Milk from Bantry:
          yellow cream floating
          on silky white.
My stomach surged
          as I held the cold bottle

and sipped. Taste of bone,
          animal and clean,
then lichen,
          parsley, bracken.
Neither sweet nor bitter.

After so long hungry
          each suck felt obscene.
I'd needed nothing
          not even green juice
          from new lettuce or melons.

Now a cream-drinker –
          my body guides me
          again and again
to the fridge's butter-square of light.

Buddleia

I'm not saying I had penis envy
but I'm also not *not* saying that –
there I was, soft-hipped, skin
twitching with nerves, dreaming myself
into a naval vessel's rigging,
a sword at my hip. Or with a motorbike
pulsing under me, cigarette
pinched in my lips. Or wandering
tough as a bulldog in the midnight park
smelling almond blossom and beer
as I picked up men. I did sleep with one –
his cock disappointed me: hot
and wrinkled, like a small mammal,
a mole. It seemed easily bruised.
The night my grandmother died
he explained the tensile strength
of metal until I stopped crying.
Back home I never felt so young.
The scent of buddleia sweetened
each room, long flower stalks swayed.
Admiring their obscene silhouettes,
I realized I liked them best from a distance.

The Proof

Tasting her still, I'd walk home
in smog, frost, past burnt-out cars,
and under bridges, as though the night
was safer than her bed.
As I squat in the boggy grass
somewhere above Baltinglass,
I see myself as I was then, braced
against wind in the underpass,
wearing a thin black coat, and trainers
that never dried. Here too,
between the Sitka spruce,
everything is wet. Mist
pimples my two flanks,
steam rises from my piss,
smells hot and animal, at home
with the mushrooms and the sheep
tugging grass. The valley echoes
inside the November cloud.
I've learned I can't protect myself,
that I'm always open. I yield,
drop by drop. Unsteady now,
I stand up, a little muddier,
make my way to the car, to the person
I trust to wait for me.

Pride 2017

Summer solstice,
we lie without covers,
room scented by buddleia.

Our new rings gleam.
This is old as kissing –
two bodies of the same kind

loving one another. We are new
because promises we made bind us
in law as well as love.

At the close of the Soviet Union,
we were born: you on the Polish border,
I by Scotsman's Bay.

We didn't know it was the right time –
strangers already marched for us.
In bitter years of boys' hands up our shirts,

our names on bus stops and walls,
we didn't know our luck:
that we would find this moment

when we sleep safe
this shortest night,
and wake to a rainstorm,

frogs leaping in yarrow and lady's bedstraw.

We Lose Our Edges

For hours after I undress
I'm marked by the gnaw
of my clothes. My bra
a toothless mouth
gumming my torso,
my stomach chewed
into red ridges.
Now I unpack you too,
taste the sweat
between your breasts,
the soft black hair
on your lower back.
You are criss-crossed
with buttons, elastic.
Outside: bees, a crow,
piano scales.
The heat gathers
against the windows
like a fin whale lying
on our walls.
Without clothes our skin
loses its edges
the way in deep water
jellyfish look as ornate
as chandeliers
but become slick stains
when they're thrown
on the beach

and we give ourselves to salt.
I can't read the words
in your skull,
just the throb of your heat
against my thumb bone
and how your eyes open
as the fin whale passes,
as the roof
over our heads
dissolves.

When My Wife Is ...

A Snail

when   my   wife   is   a   snail
nothing   is   so   important
    she   can't   put it off   until   after eleven

until she's   d   o   z   e   d
    nibbled   a   tulip bulb
        nudged   an earthworm

nothing   is   too small
for her   attention –
    a pebble   thread of a root
    condensation   on the water butt
    air   thinning   as   rain stops

eyes   slide
    over her   as   though   she   doesn't exist
but I   spotted her   in the brown shade
tentacles   under her eyestalks   tasting my sweat   on the breeze

her whole body   soft   as the inside   of my mouth
    I stay   s   t   i   l   l

her   wet   teeth   on   my skin
    consider   my   every   part
    until   we   are
q   u   i   v   e   r   i   n   g

A Witch

When my wife is a witch
she takes foxes as familiars.
They're angry, full of mange and lice,
calls pulsing like engines
under our window.

She feeds them from her thigh,
a spot that grows numb and bloodless.
As I drowse beside her, I smell
burnt rubber, long-dead mouse –
fox. When I wake, she's watching me,

her eyes silver as teaspoons,
and I need so much
I grow many mouths –
a doe-mouth, drooling,
a pheasant-mouth, begging,

a calf-mouth, crushing,
a salmon-mouth, sighing. She says
I remind her of caves fringed in lichen,
of squirming insects that thrive
in the dark. She soothes me

with lips that taste of soil.
She longs for autumn –
I'm the acid in her guts;
together we guide the moon
to her sweet rhythm.

A Walrus

When my wife is a walrus,
summer is one stretch of light.
She sings and barks with the others
on the pack ice, and in that moment,
Greenland is eternal. No hunters
come to carve her ivory into shoehorns,
billiard balls or cribbage boards.
In each polynya, the sea remains black
and cold, and ice always thickens
across the gulfs. Hungry,
she whiskers the ocean's floor,
finding oysters and bivalves.
Afterwards, she hauls herself up
to tenderly rub moustaches with me. Brine
catches in her prickles as we knock tusks.
Her tonne of blubber joins mine
in a rush of flippers, her eyes
shining squid-ink dark.

A Hazel Tree

When my wife is a hazel tree
she holds her own in the bramble hedge
though wind-rusted and jagged.
She thrives on borders
where streams split the hills;
she stands as a sentry between fields.
In her, small birds nest – goldcrests,
dunnocks. Badgers burrow in her roots.
Her shoots escort me on cold night walks,
protect me from red-eyed pigs
or ghosts straddling my shoulders.
I consume her by handfuls,
easing open her shells.
As I sleep, I hear leaves move.
I fear for her – she grows untended,
is vulnerable to strimmers and billhooks.
She spends winter glowing with cold.

A Werewolf

When my wife is a werewolf
she licks my scars. Her tongue
deciphers the raised lines.
She doesn't ask: she knows
fear festered in my guts
until I had to cut it out.
She understands –
she grows fur in moonlight,
teeth her gums can't contain.
All night, she howls,
longing to silence
a deer's pulse
with a jerk of her jaw,
or to tear a man's throat.
She belongs
with jagged shadows
sharing a kill. When she holds me
I feel the length of her claws
against my back.
She could rend ribs.
I bury my nose in her fur,
smell a peat river,
bitter tea. I am small
as a rabbit against her
yet I feel huge
as the forest she longs for.

Sheep's Head Peninsula

As I lie on my back in the dry grass
I watch bats disturb the stars. The night
tastes of summer clams and dock leaves,
bats overhead taste flies and moths
with their snouts and wings.
I picture the word *bat* printed on a page –
it's all wrong, bat is movement, a flicker
that for a moment erases part of the night.
        So many words are wrong:
        the closed letters of *dog* – dog
        is snout and paw against my leg;
        the heaviness of *home* – home is circles
        joining. Sign was the first language:
        before blurred lips began to speak
        we opened our hands to invent
        a new world. I know this as I know night
        is better when words are erased,
        replaced by stars, and bats, and you.

The Drey

When the squirrel stands
     on her hind paws,
I see a pink line
     of swollen nipples.

Nearby
     there must be a drey
of babies waiting
     to sup her milk.

As I watch her
     I realize everything
I love
     is grey –

birches whispering
     to me all night
as they break the wall
     with hungry roots;

my mother,
     silvery in evening light
as she tugs
     weed from the pond;

the newt, a band
     of muscle and movement
she stoops to return
     to colourless water;

even Milena is grey
        at the temples,
eyes shadowed
        as she lies by me in bed

with the pewter cat
        who nudges a space
between our torsos,
        and rasps a purr.

When rain starts,
        I smell lavender and soil
and for a moment
        I am the squirrel

on the trellis, unpeeling
        dove-grey sunflower seeds
to turn
        into sweet milk.

Notes

'The Light Comes in the Name of the Voice'
The title is a statement made by Jeanne d'Arc at her trial, and is quoted by Anne Carson in her essay 'Variations on the Right to Remain Silent'.

'I Mapped the Heavens'
Caroline Herschel (1750– 1848), along with her brother, William, was one of the most important astronomers of the 19th century. She was the first woman to discover a comet, and her astronomical charts were invaluable to future astronomers. In 1828 she was awarded the Gold Medal of the Royal Astronomical Society; no woman would receive one again for 168 years.

'Dörchen'
Dora Richter (1891–1933), was a domestic servant, and the first person to receive MTF gender affirmation surgery, at Berlin's Institute for Sexual Research.

'Ursa Major'
Władysław Zwolak (1924–1980), like many Polish people, was transported to a Siberian Gulag for an unknown crime. He escaped and survived a gruelling journey home to reunite with his family. My wife, Władysław's granddaughter, says the circumstances of his escape and journey were rarely discussed.

'Sheep's Head Peninsula'
The signs for *dog* and *home* described here are those used in Irish Sign Language.

Acknowledgements

My thanks to the editors of the following journals, websites and anthologies, in which some of these poems have previously appeared, sometimes in a different form: *Agenda, Banshee, Butcher's Dog, Dream of the River* (Jacar Press), *Fourteen Poems*, HeadStuff.org, *Impossible Archetype*, LambdaLiterary.org, TheLearnedPig.org, *The London Magazine, Multiverse: An International Anthology of Science Fiction Poetry* (Shoreline of Infinity), *Magma Poetry, The Ogham Stone, The Rialto, The Penny Dreadful, Poetry Ireland Review, Poetry Jukebox, Poetry Salzburg Review,* and *Queering the Green: Post-2000 Queer Irish Poetry* (The Lifeboat Press).

Many thanks to the Banshees, Laura Cassidy, Claire Hennessy and Eimear Ryan, for the attention, dedication and care they give all the work they publish, including my own. Heartfelt thanks to Annemarie Ní Churreáin, who so insightfully edited this manuscript; to Jane Clarke, Eithne Hand, Catherine Phil MacCarthy and Jessica Traynor for their invaluable support, encouragement and discerning eyes; to teachers and fellow students at the Poetry School, London (2020–1); and to Words Ireland, DLR Arts Office and Enda Wyley for the Mentorship in 2019. I'm very grateful for the guidance and kindness Paul Maddern has given me, long past the remit of the Mairtín Crawford Award. Thanks also, to dear friends in poetry and writing, and wonderful allies, Elizabeth Beaton, Anna Bowles and Rachel Plummer. Special thanks to Bronwyn Wallace for introducing me to Sylvia Townsend Warner, and to so many other witches. Love to my mother, Kilda Taylor – for her fierce support, her unfailing belief, and for her excellent grammatical advice, most of which I ignored. And to my wife, Milena Taylor – there are no words, but I've done my best in these poems.

BANSHEE
PRESS

Banshee Press was founded by writers Laura Cassidy, Claire Hennessy and Eimear Ryan. Since 2015, they have published *Banshee* literary journal twice a year. The Banshee Press publishing imprint launched in 2019. Titles include *Paris Syndrome* by Lucy Sweeney Byrne, *Gold Light Shining* by Bebe Ashley, and *I Want to Know That I Will Be Okay* by Deirdre Sullivan.

WWW.BANSHEELIT.COM